D0764092

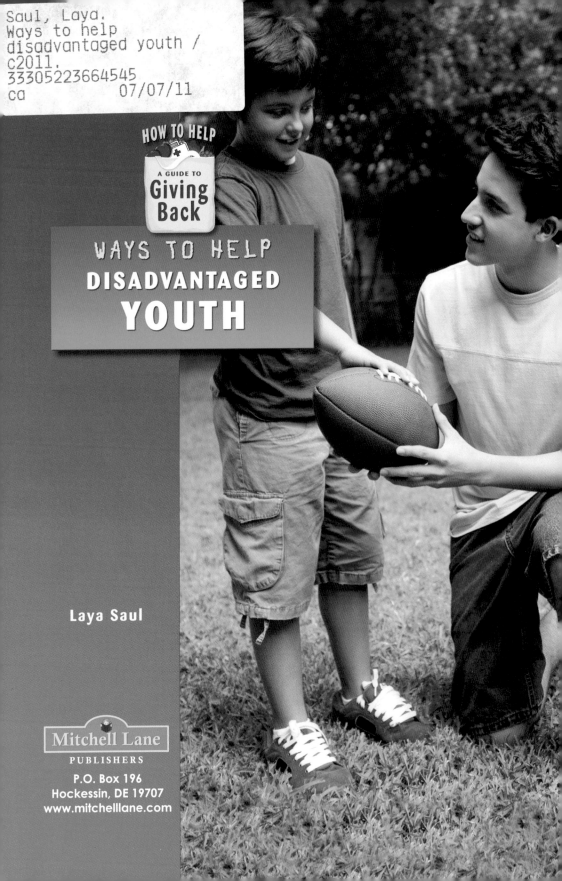

Saul, Laya.
Ways to help
disadvantaged youth /
c2011.
33305223664545
ca   07/07/11

HOW TO HELP
A GUIDE TO
Giving
Back

WAYS TO HELP
DISADVANTAGED
YOUTH

Laya Saul

Mitchell Lane
PUBLISHERS
P.O. Box 196
Hockessin, DE 19707
www.mitchelllane.com

Ways to Help After a Natural Disaster
Ways to Help Children With Disabilities
Ways to Help Chronically Ill Children
Ways to Help Disadvantaged Youth
Ways to Help in Your Community
Ways to Help the Elderly
Volunteering in Your School
Celebrities Giving Back

Copyright © 2011 by Mitchell Lane Publishers

All rights reserved. No part of this book may be reproduced without written permission from the publisher. Printed and bound in the United States of America.

PUBLISHER'S NOTE: The facts on which the story in this book is based have been thoroughly researched. Documentation of such research can be found on page 46. While every possible effort has been made to ensure accuracy, the publisher will not assume liability for damages caused by inaccuracies in the data, and makes no warranty on the accuracy of the information contained herein.

Library of Congress
Cataloging-in-Publication Data

Saul, Laya.
  Ways to help disadvantaged youth / by Laya Saul.
      p. cm. — (How to help : a guide to giving back)
  Includes bibliographical references and index.
  ISBN 978-1-58415-918-6 (library bound)
  1. Poor youth—Juvenile literature. 2. Youth with social disabilities—Juvenile literature. I. Title.
  HV1421.S38 2011
  362.74—dc22
                                              2010006536

Printing   1   2   3   4   5   6   7   8   9

                                                    PLB

CONTENTS

Introduction:
Making a Real Difference

James's family can afford to pay for all the hockey uniforms and equipment he needs. Michael's mom taught him how to study effectively and that it is important to do his homework each day. Susan lives in a well-kept neighborhood where all the kids shop at top department stores. Keisha's dad is an executive who loves to challenge her thoughts at the dinner table each night. These four kids have wonderful advantages in life. But not everyone is born into a home with parents who have the resources to take good care of their kids. Some families live in poverty, and they must make finding their next meal their top priority.

For a child who lives at or below the poverty level, the family might not have the money to buy new clothes. They may have to decide whether they will pay their phone bill, have electricity, or buy food for that week. A child's family may not have a home at all.

Some children come from homes that were not safe. They may have been abused or neglected—meaning that the people who were supposed to love and protect them hurt

them or ignored them in a way that hurt them. These kids were removed from their homes and placed in foster care.

Some children come from loving homes but their parents do not have the advantage of education. Parents who cannot read, for example, can't help their children learn how to read.

Everyone has something hard about his or her life, but some children face more difficulties than others. You can make a difference in the life of a child who does not have the same advantages that many others take for granted.

Dignity
Perhaps you would like to help disadvantaged kids stay warm in the winter. You might think that it's better to be warm in an old, stained coat than to freeze with no coat at all. Yet I'm sure you can imagine how embarrassed someone would feel to show up to school or work in a coat that was stained, ripped, or didn't fit properly. Some kids would rather be cold than feel humiliated.

A Girl Scout troop and other volunteers in Western New York collected several hundred pounds of used clothing for people in need.

We all want to know that any gift—whether it is time, money, or a piece of clothing—is going to be appreciated. It is important to give in a way that protects the dignity of the person who receives your gift.

Understanding

Many of the children who fall in the disadvantaged category have had to face big challenges. They might not have had anyone to teach them about gratitude, and so they may not know how to accept good things graciously. They may be so emotionally hurt that their hearts are closed off to your help. Give anyway. Just make sure you are giving from a place that is sincere. Don't get mad and don't give up if things don't work out the way you wanted. Kindness is like water in a fountain. It cycles around. Even if it looks as if your kind acts were not well received, the truth of your kindness will still light up the world. Who knows, it may be your open heart that makes the biggest difference—even more than the actual project you choose as the vehicle for your giving.

Boundaries

Another thing to think about when giving is just how much you have to give. What are your boundaries? A boundary is like the fence around your yard that keeps your pet dog in, safe from getting hit by a car, and keeps stray animals out. Giving means you give what you can but you still have a boundary; you know where the line is, so you are also taking care of yourself. Not everyone knows how to respect a boundary, so you need to know where yours is, and make sure that you honor your own limits. No one person can fix the world; we each just have to do our part.

Students from Florida's Shorecrest School held a clothing drive for the girls of Brookwood, Florida. The goods are on their way!

Have patience when tutoring someone.

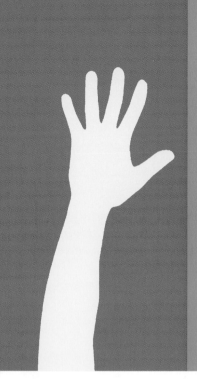

Chapter 1

Be a Tutor

A child can have learning challenges for any number of reasons, and there might be no one available to help.

Helping one young person to succeed in school can make a world of difference. As the saying goes, "You may be just one person in the world, but you can mean the world to one person."

What are your strengths? Do you love reading? Are you comfortable with math? Some students have parents who don't speak English, so it is impossible for them to help their children with schoolwork. A child can have learning challenges for any number of reasons, and there might be no one available to help.

When you teach someone how to read or understand the puzzles of math, you give him or her a gift that lasts a lifetime. Not only are you helping a person strengthen a skill, you may also be helping build that person's confidence that he or she can succeed.

Patience is the top tool you'll need in working with someone who is struggling in school. With your enthusiastic encouragement, the child you work with will build the courage to keep trying.

Struggling to read can be so discouraging. Helping a child to master reading is a lifelong gift.

Here are some other tools you can use when sharing the gift of reading:

- Programs at the public library; you can also try your school library
- Literacy games online
- Books such as *Teach Your Child to Read in 100 Easy Lessons* can be used over months to help someone become a reader—the whole process is scripted for you

Just because someone can't read or do math or is weak in any other subject does not mean that person is not smart; it means no one has been able to take the time to teach in a way that he or she can understand.

Once a young man in his twenties came to a public library to ask for help in reading. As he continued in his lessons, he told his tutor that his mother always talked about how slow and dumb he was. He believed her and did not even try. Today that man can read!

Chapter 2

Hold a Book Drive

You can take the books you collect to an organization that works with disadvantaged children.

You may want to help someone learn how to read, or you may want to collect books that children or teens will enjoy reading. You can take the books you collect to an organization that works with disadvantaged children.

Ways to Get Books

Contact children's book publishers. Call or write letters to publishers asking them if they would like to donate books for your charity. You can even include a copy of a letter from the program with which you are working. To find a list of publishers, look in *Children's Writer's and Illustrator's Market*, which you can probably find in your local library in the reference section.

Ask your local library if they would give you books in good condition that are being withdrawn or that people have donated to the library.

Tell the people you know—your neighbors, family, friends, work associates, and people from any organization you are in—that you are collecting books for disadvantaged kids.

The Marine Toys for Tots program collects books as well as toys. Each year this organization distributes thousands of gifts to disadvantaged children.

Other organizations will use donated money to purchase and distribute books to disadvantaged children, such as the Marine Toys for Tots Literacy Program. You can also contact your local library to find out about literacy projects in your area.

There are other organizations that would love to have new or gently used books. Kids In Need—Books In Deed will let you send the books you collect directly where they are needed. They will also teach you how to organize a write-a-thon at your school to raise money for literacy programs.

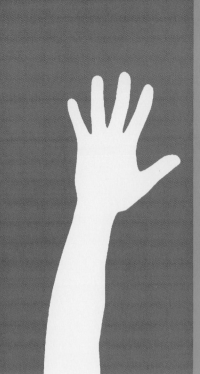

Chapter **3**

Go Green with Kids

If you have a green thumb, there are ways you can promote green living and give some kids a chance to blossom too!

It's a wonderful feeling to plant something and watch it grow. If you have a green thumb, there are ways you can promote green living and give some kids a chance to blossom too!

Find a program that works with disadvantaged kids in your area. You could call a local social services office in your area or look in the phone book to find a youth placement facility in your area that takes volunteers. Social services are government offices designed to help people. They are often overburdened with work, so when you reach someone, explain what you want to do and politely ask for names and numbers of organizations or children's homes in your area where you could volunteer.

Then, call the home or organization and ask to speak with the person who handles volunteer opportunities. Explain that you would like to volunteer to do a special workshop for kids on gardening.

Have a Plan

Work out plans for your garden and write them down. Writing them down shows that you have carefully thought about what you are doing and that you are committed to the project. It also makes things go smoother for you when you show up to volunteer. You'll be certain to have all the supplies you need, and you'll know what to do and when.

What will you grow? Do you want to grow flowers or vegetables or both, and what kinds? Once you know what you're growing, determine the supplies you'll need. Here's a possible list:

- location: a place that gets sun or shade where you can do some digging and planting (you might also consider container gardening)
- tools: shovels, spades, gloves, hoses
- soil, fertilizer, compost, pots
- seeds or seedlings
- plant markers and string (for keeping track of where you plant)

Who will pay for the supplies? Some organizations have budgets for seeds, seedlings, fertilizer, and other supplies you'll need. Some places may even have tools and other supplies that you can borrow.

Who will be involved? Will it be just you or will you come with a group? How many children can participate in the garden project?

Work out a schedule. How many times a week will you come to work with the children? How long will you spend with them each time you come? How long from the time you plant until the flowers bloom or the vegetables are ready to eat?

You'll be growing more than vegetables when you help kids experience the wonder and delight of a vegetable or flower garden.

How will you finish the project? Will the kids make soup or salsa with the vegetables you grow? Will they bring the flowers to a hospital or use them to decorate their dining room?

You can show the kids that each kind of plant—just like each person—needs something a little different to grow at its best. Some need more sun and some need more shade, for example. Help them notice that even though you plant a bunch of seeds at the same time, they each bloom at different times—just like people!

Students at Emmanuel Middle School organized a fund-raiser by having everyone wear colorful stripes for the day. They also raffled off toys and held a talent show.

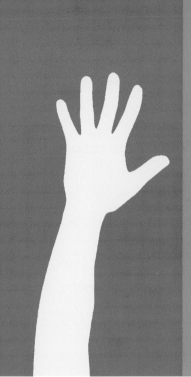

Chapter 4

Help by Fund-raising

In choosing a charity, be sure you have checked to make sure it is honest.

There are many worthy charities doing great things. Some work locally, some nationally, and some internationally for a whole spectrum of causes.

In choosing a charity, be sure you have checked to make sure it is honest. People who say they are collecting for charity but are really not putting the money where they say can seem very friendly and even likable. There are web sites that rate the honesty of charities. For example, Charity Navigator (http://www.charitynavigator.org) will let you search the charity you're thinking about to see the rating, or you can sort charities by location, type, and rating to get ideas of where to donate. Also useful are Guidestar Nonprofit Reports (http://www2.guidestar.org/) and the American Institute of Philanthropy (http://charitywatch.org/).

Not every charity is listed. Just because you don't see it on a list does not mean it's not a good organization. Ask adults you know to help you research if you're not sure.

When you find a charity or project and decide that fund-raising is how you want to help, here are some ideas.

Raffle Party

A raffle party is easier to do with a team, so maybe your class or club can organize this together. You'll need to ask people who own businesses or sell products to donate various goods to use as prizes. Prizes can be anything from a coupon for food, ice cream, or coffee to jewelry, books, electronics, or a service (such as a massage, consultation, or haircut).

Here's what you'll need:

- A letter to give to business owners explaining the project and the cause
- A place for the raffle party
- Raffle tickets—you can buy or make these
- Cash box or some other place to put the money you collect
- List of businesses and people who donated a prize
- Thank-you notes for prize donors

Here's a checklist of things to do:

- √ Decide on the charity you want to support.
- √ Choose a date to have your raffle party.
- √ Set realistic goals: the amount you want to raise; the number of people you'd like to attend.
- √ Find a location for the party—you may be able to use a rec room, school facility, or church social hall.
- √ Collect prizes.
- √ Decorate the room.
- √ Set up tables with the prizes; next to each prize, place a small can or box to collect the raffle tickets.
- √ At another table, sell raffle tickets for a set price.

Bake sales are a sweet way to raise cash.

√ Have a speaker there (or you can do this!) to let the guests know how their money is helping disadvantaged youth.

√ Draw a raffle ticket for each prize and hand them to the winners.

Put Together a Cookbook

Putting together a cookbook can be fun. You could do this in your school or through your church or parents' place of work. Ask everyone to contribute a favorite, original recipe. There are companies that will publish all the recipes in a book, which you can then sell to raise money for the charity or for a project you are trying to put together. Once you've collected the recipes, you can begin to take orders and sell the book. Be sure to ask all the people who contribute a recipe if they would like to buy a copy to help the cause. You could give the book a theme to make it more interesting, like soups and salads or entertaining guests or even holiday recipes.

Other Ideas

Be creative. You can do something basic like a car wash or bake sale, or research how money can be raised from getting people to donate other things like cars, mileage points, and even shopping online. If you come up with an idea that's not listed in this book, ask around and see if you can make your own creative ideas happen.

Nutritious kid-friendly foods such as applesauce, cereal, and macaroni and cheese make great food drive donations.

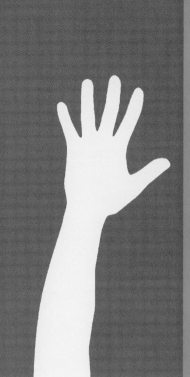

Chapter 5

Hold a Food Drive

Bring comfort and better health to children and families who need it.

Anthony Robbins is a world-renowned teacher in the field of self-improvement and motivation. Every year at Thanksgiving, he launches a big campaign to provide families with food. He explains why he is passionate about this when he tells his story. As a child, his family was very poor, and there were problems in the home. One Thanksgiving Day, someone knocked on their door, bringing them a box of food that was full of everything they would need to have a Thanksgiving feast. Even now, as a multimillionaire, his eyes brim over and he gets choked up as he tells the story of the moment that changed his life: knowing that a stranger cared enough to bring such a gift.

At the age of seventeen, he quietly started to pay it forward by bringing baskets of food to two families at Thanksgiving. Each year he doubled the number of families he helped, and eventually he asked some friends to pitch in. This project grew over the years until it became a foundation. He continues this work, and over thirty years later feeds

millions of people internationally. Robbins advises, "Reach out and touch a stranger for no other reason than because it's right! It will give your life meaning."[1]

Sometimes your local grocery store will put out containers to collect food. Scouting groups and postal carriers have regular food drives, too.

Choose an organization that will distribute the food, and get their list of suggested donations. They will probably list foods that won't go bad, such as canned foods (vegetables, fish, fruit), dry foods (pasta, rice, crackers), and jarred foods (peanut butter, jelly, pasta sauce). You can print the list to show the people who are donating. When you donate money to the organizations that distribute the food, they can add fresh fruits and vegetables, breads, or meats.

People always need to eat, every day all year long, and there are hungry people all around the world. This is a project that will bring comfort and even better health to children and families who need it.

Have fun advertising your food drive. Be as creative as you want!

1. Anthony Robbins, "Five Keys to Thrive," *Change Your Life Now* (video), http://training.tonyrobbins.com/?p=378

Chapter 6

Hold a Toy Drive

For many kids in the United States and around the globe, it may be beyond their wildest dreams to receive a new toy.

Did you have a favorite stuffed animal that was your constant bedtime buddy? When you were really young, the toy might have been a doll or an action figure or a new game. When you got older, the "toys" might have been electronics or maybe new music or some cash. For many kids in the United States and around the globe, it may be beyond their wildest dreams to receive a new toy. Now imagine that you are responsible for giving toys to kids who, without your help, would go without.

Most people have a soft spot for bringing a new gift to children during the Christmas or Hanukkah season. The best-known organization for collecting and distributing toys for disadvantaged children is Toys for Tots.

You can sponsor a toy drive of your own and then donate the toys you collect. If you go to the donation page at the Toys for Tots web site and click on your state, then either your city or county, you'll get connected with the local campaign office or learn where the nearest drop-off site is in your area. Toys should be new, in their original packaging, and not wrapped.

The Police Athletic League (PAL) organizes sports events for disadvantaged youth, such as trips to see the Harlem Globetrotters. You could have a drive to collect sports equipment for your local PAL office.

An established and reputable organization is a great way to go, but you can get more personal if you are willing to do a bit more work. For example, you could deliver your donations directly to organizations that service disadvantaged children, such as the Police Athletic League.

While a toy can bring joy to the heart of a child, the memory of receiving that toy, of knowing that someone cares and the comfort that can bring, can last a lifetime.

Something to Consider
When you are older, you may be just the right kind of person to give more by becoming a Big Brother or Big Sister to a child who needs the attention and affection of a caring adult. In as little as a few hours a week (maybe less), you can help a child grow up to know that he or she is lovable. This simple gift of time can help someone become a healthier or more successful adult.

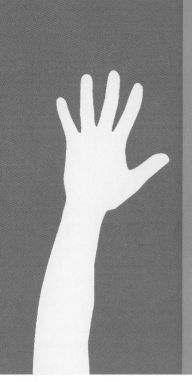

Stuff a Duffel

The starting point is gathering duffel bags or backpacks for filling with the gifts you collect.

When Annie Wignall was eleven years old, she learned about kids in crisis who had to leave home with very few belongings. She started a small project to get a few children a bag of goodies—useful things as well as comfort items. The idea was to help one child at a time.

What started with one girl who had an idea and shared that idea became the Care Bags Foundation (Care Bags 4 Kids). This nationally recognized nonprofit helps thousands of children around the world.

You can start your own project by donating bags of goodies through a local social services office, or by joining Care Bags 4 Kids.

Ask People You Know for Donations

Send an e-mail or print a letter asking people to donate new things from a list you either make yourself or download from Care Bags 4 Kids. The starting point is gathering duffel bags or backpacks for filling with the gifts you collect. The donations can be for any age, for boys or girls. You can also suggest that people make blankets (or quillows—a blanket in its own

bag that doubles as a pillow), bibs, or bags to hold all the goodies.

What to Include

The things you include in your bags must all be new, in their original packaging, and there should be no breakables (like glass). Include basic items, such as toiletries (toothbrush, toothpaste, lotion, shampoo) and comfort items (quilts, stuffed animals, or books). You might also want to include things like art supplies, stickers, cards, or diaries, depending on the age of the recipient. Since some people have food allergies or other restrictions, there should never be food items in the bags.

Quick-Start Ideas

For a fast start, go to the Care Bags 4 Kids web site (http://www.carebags4kids.org) and download their lists and ideas. Then click on the "about us" link for detailed information about how to work with them. You can also contact a local social services office to learn about the needs in your own community.

Donation Station

If you are blessed enough to have much in life, think about making your next party into a donation station. On your invitation, you can ask your guests to bring a donation of a new book, toy, food, or clothes—whatever would help the project you want to serve.

Chapter 8

Play Games

Playing games is fun, and games and puzzles actually help the brain develop, too.

Everyone likes to have fun, so why not use games for your service? There are several ways to use games to help disadvantaged youth.

Play Online

Find online games that actually make contributions to worthy causes. They are fun and easy, and you might even learn a thing or two. The way it works is that advertisers want people to know about them, so they donate money each time you play. They are hoping that after you've played for a while, you might buy one of their products. Why not support a business that tries to spend its advertising dollars to do some good at the same time?

At Free Rice (http://www.freerice.com), you can expand your vocabulary or test your math skills or chemistry knowledge when you play. Every right answer helps feed hungry people. Name that classic toy at the Back to Basics Toys web site (http://www.backtobasicstoys.com/trivia/), and the company will contribute to the purchase of new toys for disadvantaged children.

Play with Kids

You may have complete games at home that you don't play anymore because you've outgrown them. If you take them to an after-school program for disadvantaged youth, it's a casual way to make some connections and help everyone have a good time. Playing games is fun, and games and puzzles actually help the brain develop, too. Games like Set, Blokus, and Mastermind can even be played with kids who cannot read or whose reading is weak. Backgammon or Rummikub lets you have fun with numbers.

Orrin Hudson was constantly in trouble until his high school English teacher taught him the game of chess. Orrin says, "With his help, I began to understand life through a chessboard. He showed me that every move you make has consequences, and in order to improve my game and my life, I had to make better choices. I slowly realized that I was responsible for my own success or failure."[1] Now Hudson is devoted to using what he learned about the game of chess to help disadvantaged youth. He started a youth organization called Be Someone.

Host a Game Night

A third way to use games for helping is to organize a tournament or marathon. You can do this at your school, with a scouting troop, a place of worship, or any other place where people gather. You might even be able to find a toy store that would be willing to sponsor an event like this. Here's what you can do:

- Choose where you will donate your money. You could use it to buy food, books, or toys that will be donated, or give it to an organization such as Orrin Hudson's Be Someone.
- Choose the game or games to be played.

1. Be Someone: Teaching Kids That Every Move Counts,
   http://www.besomeone.org/

- Pick your date, time, and location.
- Get players to sign up. You can charge an entrance fee, which will be donated to your charity.
- Make a simple flyer to pass out to let people know about your event.
- Ask businesses to sponsor the event by donating money for the charity or prizes for winners. (The names of the businesses should be on the flyers you hand out.)
- Have fun!

You could host a simple game night, or you could organize a tournament. Winners would advance until one champion emerges.

Other Ideas

A sports equipment drive for other schools, or planning a trip to a sporting event for which you get the tickets and transportation donated (or use money from a fund-raiser) are other ideas.

Baseball star Jimmy Rollins of the Philadelphia Phillies has helped struggling families with funds raised through his Jimmy Rollins Family Foundation. He donated 32 new computers to Olney West High School in Philadelphia to create the school's first computer facility.

Chapter 9

Fun Times for All

Simple, fun times can lift spirits and give hope for a brighter future.

Many children who are disadvantaged do not get as much attention from caring adults as children with advantages. Just knowing they matter can brighten these children's lives, and having fun is a great way to relieve stress too. Simple, fun times can lift spirits and give hope for a brighter future.

Volunteer with a Youth Group

Youth groups often need volunteers. You could help a group with art projects, hiking, or organizing special trips (such as to the zoo, amusement parks, or museums). To find out which groups could use your help, contact the local offices of national scouting organizations, or contact local social services offices.

Be a Camp Counselor

Have you ever been to summer camp? There are kids for whom summer camp is a dream, and there are organizations that try to make that dream into a reality.

If you want to help give kids a memorable summer, this project could be perfect for you. While there may not be many opportunities for sleepaway camps for disadvantaged youth, with a bit of research you should be able to find a day camp for inner-city kids where your help would be appreciated. Sometimes organizations (such as a local police department) will sponsor a special camp, and sometimes camps give scholarships. Here's where any fund-raising efforts could come in handy—you could help pay for others to have a camping experience.

Organize a Mini Carnival
Throwing a mini carnival is a great idea for kids aged four to nine. You'll need to do this project with a large group of volunteers. It will take some work, but it will bring great memories for the children who attend. You could also use this event as a fund-raiser and donate the money to your favorite charity.

Here's what to do:
- √ Make a list of some simple carnival games or activities:
  - bean bag toss (through a target)
  - T-ball toss (knock over tin cans you decorate)
  - rubber duck pick (number them for prizes)
  - balloon stomp (with paper inside listing prizes)
  - art pavilion (stocked for a few craft projects)
  - snack area
  - face painting (you can ask someone in a local department store if there is a makeup artist who would want to volunteer)
- √ Make a list of what you'll need for each game or activity (have an extra game or two in mind and some extra supplies). Remember trash bags for cleanup.

√ Purchase prizes and game tickets (you can also make these or ask for them to be donated).
√ Set a time, date, and location of your carnival.
√ Make sure you have all the permissions you need from the school or other group for the time, place, and equipment you'll use.
√ Organize volunteers to run each game, to sell or pass out tickets, and to clean up.
√ Have fun!

The Punahou School carnival has become an annual tradition in Hawaii. The largest fundraising carnival in the state, it pays for student financial aid. One of the most heralded beneficiaries? President Barack Obama.

Peer counseling is a way of helping people get through the hard times in life—of letting them know they are not alone.

Chapter 10

Offer Peer Counseling

It can be comforting just to know that someone else understands.

Peer counseling is a service for anyone in a difficult situation who needs advice or just someone to talk to. A peer counselor is someone who is in the same position as the one being counseled. For this situation, it means a young adult or teen is counseling another teen. It does not mean you have to have had the same problems.

Peer counseling can be helpful in a number of ways. In some peer counseling programs, a student helps a new student get settled in school, register for classes, and find his or her way around. Other times, a teen can talk with someone else his or her age about the problems he or she is facing. So many people feel like they are alone in their struggles, and it can be comforting just to know that someone else understands. Mediation is another form of peer counseling. With some training in problem-solving skills (which is often available through school programs), mediators help people in a disagreement reach a compromise.

Peer counseling should be done with supervision. You should not be in it alone. Your school counseling department may provide training opportunities, and you should take advantage of any other types of training you can to help you help others. Peer counseling requires serious commitment.

The topics of peer counseling range from extending friendship to those who are very shy to educating others about how to deal with difficult issues such as child abuse, drug abuse, or HIV/AIDS. While these important issues affect people from every economic background, disadvantaged kids may not have the same resources available to them as other youths. They may not know where else to turn.

There are web sites available where teens counsel teens, and you can volunteer to work with one of those. Some of them require that the counselor be at least 15 or 16 years old. Online or telephone counseling also requires training by the sponsoring organization.

To be a counselor, you should be a good listener. Sometimes just being heard is a relief and in itself can be healing. You should be able to "reflect" what people share by repeating some of the things they say. In the same way that a mirror reflects, repetition lets the speaker know that he or she is being heard, that you care enough to really listen. You should also have professional resources at your fingertips. Some kids are dealing with very frightening or dangerous situations in their lives. Have a list of agencies you can call for help: hotline phone numbers, counselors, and organizations that allow callers to remain anonymous. You can photocopy the list of organizations on page 38 to keep near your phone. Be sure to add local agencies as well.

It is no small thing to help someone feel noticed and cared for. The skills you will develop as a peer counselor can benefit you as well. You will learn about and experience feeling for other people, and you will also develop good communication skills.

Please note: If someone talks with you about something dangerous that is happening—if someone is getting hurt or could get hurt—it is important that you speak with a reliable and competent adult who can step in and take over. Keeping a person's information confidential is important in nearly every situation, but saving a life is most important of all. If your adviser is not available and you need to make a decision, call a hotline and ask a counselor for advice. If the danger is immediate, call 9-1-1.

Your adult adviser: _____ Phone number:_____

Alternate adviser: _____ Phone number:_____

Local police:_____ Phone number:_____

Local hospital: _____ Phone number:_____

Service Referrals

Alcoholism
Al-Anon and Alateen
http://www.al-anon.alateen.org

Alcoholics Anonymous
http://www.aa.org

Drug Abuse
Narcotics Anonymous
http://www.na.org

Eating Disorders
Caring Online
http://www.caringonline.com

Overeaters Anonymous
http://www.oa.org

Self-harm
Recover Your Life: Self-Harm
Support Community and
Information
http://www.recoveryourlife.com

Sexual Abuse
Childhelp
1-800-4-A-CHILD (1-800-422-4453)
http://www.childhelp.org

Stop It Now!
http://www.stopitnow.com

National Sexual Assault Hotline
1.800.656.HOPE (4673)
http://www.rainn.org
(click on "Get Help")

Suicide Prevention
Hopeline
1-800-SUICIDE (1-800-784-2433)
http://www.hopeline.com
(click on "Get Help Now")

National Suicide Prevention Hotline
1-800-273-TALK (1-800-273-8255)
http://www.suicidepreventionlifeline.
org

YAH! Youth America Hotline
1-877-YOUTHLINE (1-877-9688-454)
http://www.youthline.us

Other Issues
Covenant House: Nineline
1-800-999-9999
http://www.nineline.org

National Organization for Victim
Assistance
http://www.trynova.org

Teen Help
http://www.teenhelp.org

This page is reproducible for distribution but not for resale.
Copyright © 2011 by Mitchell Lane Publishers.

Whether you serve as a camp counselor, peer counselor, or organizer for fund-raisers, putting a smile on a child's face is a heartwarming reward for volunteering.

A Little More to Think About

Whatever project you work on is sure to touch lives. Be sure to let your friends and family know what you are doing through e-mail and through any online networking sites you use so that they can help and support you.

There's a story of a man who walked along a beach where hundreds of starfish were washed ashore. As he walked, he would stop, pick up a starfish, and then toss it into the sea. Another man said to him, "Do you think what you're doing here really makes a difference?" Silently, the first man picked up another starfish. As he tossed it into the water, he answered, "It did to that one!"

National Organizations

Be Someone: Teaching Kids That Every
Move Counts
http://www.besomeone.org/

Big Brothers Big Sisters of America
http://www.bbbs.org/

Books for America
http://www.booksforamerica.org/

Care Bags Foundation
http://www.carebags4kids.org

Kids Helping Kids
http://kidzhelpingkids.org

Kids in Need—Books in Deed
http://www.booksindeed.org/

Marine Toys for Tots Literacy Program
http://www.toysfortots.org/literacy/

National Association of Police Athletic/
Activities Leagues (PAL)
http://www.nationalpal.org/

Project Night Light
http://www.projectnightnight.org/

United Way
http://national.unitedway.org/volunteer/
youth.cfm

Alabama

Alabama Baptist Children's Homes
P.O. Box 361767
Birmingham, AL 35236
Phone: (205) 982-1112
Toll Free: (888) 720-8805
http://www.abchome.org/

Penelope House
P.O. Box 9127
Mobile, AL 36691
Phone: (251) 342-2809
http://www.penelopehouse.org/

Alaska

Ascent Russian Orphan Aid Foundation
P.O. Box 1305
Palmer, AK 99645
Phone: (415) 367-3500
http://www.iorphan.org

Covenant House Alaska
609 F Street
Anchorage, AK 99501
Phone: (907) 272-1255
http://covenanthouseak.org/

Arizona

Childhelp Info Center: Childhelp, Inc.
15757 North 78th Street
Scottsdale, AZ 85260
Phone: (480) 922-8212
http://childhelpinfocenter.org/

Healing Hearts for Children's Hearts
1855 E. Northern, Suite 202
Phoenix, AZ 85020
Phone: (602) 861-6735
http://www.azcac.org/

Arkansas

Children's Homes Inc.
5515 Walcott Road
Paragould, AR 72450
Phone: (870) 239-4031
Toll Free: (800) 382-4114
www.childrenshomes.org

Northwest Arkansas Children's Shelter
7702 SW Regional Airport Blvd.
Bentonville, AR 72712
Phone: (479) 795-2417
http://www.nwacs.com/

California

Homeless Children's Network
3265 17th Street, Suite 404
San Francisco, CA 94110
Phone: (415) 437-3990
http://www.hcnkids.org/

Orangewood Children's Foundation
1575 E. 17th Street
Santa Ana, CA 92705
Phone: (714) 619-0200
http://www.orangewoodfoundation.org/

Colorado

Salvation Army of Colorado Springs
908 Yuma Street
Colorado Springs, CO 80909
Phone: (719) 636-3891
http://www.tsacs.org/

The Women's Crisis/Family Outreach Center
P.O. Box 367
Castle Rock, CO 80104
Phone: (303) 688-1094
http://www.thewomenscrisiscenter.org/

Connecticut

Boys & Girls Village, Inc.
528 Wheelers Farms Road
Milford, CT 06461
Phone: (203) 877-0300
http://www.bgvillage.org

Delaware
Homeward Bound, Inc.
Emmaus House
P.O. Box 9740
Newark, DE 19714
Phone: (302) 737-2241
http://www.homewardbound.org/

The Salvation Army in Dover
611 Forest Street
Dover, DE 19903
Phone: (302) 678-9551
http://www.salvationarmydelaware.org/

Florida
Children's Home Society of Florida
  Corporate Headquarters
1485 S. Semoran Blvd., Suite 1448
Winter Park, FL 32792
Phone: (321) 397-3000
http://www.chsfl.org/

The Shelter for Abused Women and
  Children
P.O. Box 10102
Naples, FL 34101
Phone: (239) 775-3862
http://www.naplesshelter.org/

Georgia
The Atlanta Children's Shelter
607 Peachtree Street NE
Atlanta, GA 30308
Phone: (404) 892-3713
http://www.atlantachildrensshelter.com/

Families First
P.O. Box 7948, Station C
Atlanta, GA 30357
Phone: (404) 853-2800
http://www.familiesfirst.org

Hawaii
Child & Family Service Shelter for Abused
  Spouses
200 North Vineyard Blvd., Suite 20
Honolulu, HI 96817
Phone: (808) 847-4602

Parents and Children Together
1485 Linapuni Street, Suite 105
Honolulu, HI 96819
Phone: (808) 847-3285
http://www.pacthawaii.org/contact.html

Idaho
The Children's Village, Inc.
1350 W Hanley Avenue
Coeur d'Alene, ID 83815
Phone: (208) 667-1189
http://www.thechildrensvillage.org/

Sojourners' Alliance
627 N Van Buren Street
Moscow, ID 83843
Phone: (208) 883-3438
http://www.sojournersalliance.info/

Illinois
Family Shelter Service
605 E. Roosevelt Road
Wheaton, IL 60187
Phone: (630) 221-8290
http://www.familyshelterservice.org/

Rainbow House
4149 West 26th Street
Chicago, IL 60623
Phone: (773) 521-1815
http://www.rainbow-house.org/

Indiana
Dayspring Shelter
P.O. Box 44105
Indianapolis, IN 46244
Phone: (317) 635-6780
http://www.dayspringindy.org/

Sand Castle Shelter
1005 West 8th Street
Michigan City, IN 46360
Phone: (219) 879-2552
http://www.sandcastleshelter.org

Iowa
Emergency Housing Project, Inc.
331 North Gilbert Street
Iowa City, IA 52245
Phone: (319) 351-0326

Youth & Shelter Services, Inc.
P.O. Box 1628
Ames, IA 50010
Phone: (515) 233-3141
http://www.yss.ames.ia.us

Kansas
Metropolitan Lutheran Ministry Community
  Care
722 Reynolds Avenue
Kansas City, KS 66101
Phone: (913) 342-8333

Safehome
P.O. Box 4563
Overland Park, KS 66204
Phone: (913) 432-9300
http://www.safehome-ks.org

Kentucky
Home of the Innocents
1100 East Market Street
Louisville, KY 40206
Phone: (502) 596-1029
http://www.homeoftheinnocents.org

Salvation Army of Lexington
736 West Main Street
Lexington, KY 40508
Phone: (859) 252-7706
http://www.salvationarmylex.org/

Louisiana
Salvation Army of Monroe
105 Hart Street
Monroe, LA 71201
Phone: (318) 325-1755

Society of St. Vincent de Paul
P.O. Box 127
Baton Rouge, LA 70821
Phone: (225) 383-7837
http://www.svdpbr.com/Shelter.aspx

Maine
Caring Unlimited
P.O. Box 590
Sanford, ME 04073
Phone: (207) 490-3227
http://www.caring-unlimited.org/

Salvation Army Lighthouse Shelter
297 Cumberland Avenue
Portland, ME 04101
Phone: (207) 774-3073

Maryland
Family and Children's Services
4623 Falls Road
Baltimore, MD 21209
Phone: (410) 366-1980
http://www.fcsmd.org/locations/

Hope Alive, Inc.
P.O. Box 140
Sabillasville, MD 21780
Phone: (301) 241-4005
http://www.hopealiveministries.org/

Massachusetts
Crossroads Family Shelter
56 Havre Street
East Boston, MA 02128
Phone: (617) 567-5926
http://www.ebcrossroads.org/

Temporary Home for Women and Children
41 New Chardon Street
Boston, MA 02114
Phone: (617) 720-3611
http://www.cityofboston.gov/shelter/
resources.asp?id=1

Michigan
Oakland Family Services
114 Orchard Lake Road
Pontiac, MI 48341
Phone: (248) 858-7766
http://www.oaklandfamilyservices.org/
contact.htm

SOS Community Services
101 S. Huron Street
Ypsilanti, MI 48197
Phone: (734) 485-8730
http://www.soscs.org/

Minnesota
Alexandra House
P.O. Box 49039
Blaine, MN 55449
Phone: (763) 780-2332
http://www.alexandrahouse.org/home/

Sharing and Caring Hands
525 North 7th Street
Minneapolis, MN 55405
Phone: (612) 338-4640
http://www.sharingandcaringhands.org/

Mississippi
Mississippi Children's Home Services
P.O. Box 1078
Jackson, MS 39215
Phone: (601) 969-4079
http://www.mchscares.org/

Mississippi Lighthouse Children's Home
2339 Attala Road 3111
West, MS 39192
Phone: (662) 289-9629
http://www.lighthousechildren.com/

Missouri
Rainbow House Columbia
1611 Towne Drive
Columbia, MO 65203
Phone: (573) 474-6600
http://www.rainbowhousecolumbia.org/

reSTART, Inc.
918 East 9th Street
Kansas City, MO 64106
Phone: (816) 472-5664
http://www.restartinc.org/

Montana
Montana Rescue Mission Women's & Family
    Shelter
2520 1st Avenue North
Billings, MT 59101
Phone: (406) 259-3105
http://www.montanarescuemission.org/

Watson Children's Shelter
2901 Fort Missoula Road
Missoula, MT 59804
Phone: (406) 549-0058
http://www.shelter4children.com

Nebraska
Open Door Mission
2828 North 23rd Street East
Omaha, NE 68110
Phone: (402) 422-1111
http://www.opendoormission.org/

Project Homeless Connect Omaha
747 North 148th Avenue
Omaha, NE 68154
Phone: (402) 630-5664
http://www.homelessconnectomaha.org/

Nevada
Catholic Community Services
500 E. Fourth Street
Reno, NV 89512
Phone: (775) 322-7073
http://www.ccsnn.org/

Family Promise of Reno/Sparks
P.O. Box 20988
Reno, NV 89515
Phone: (775) 284-5566
http://www.familypromisereno.com/

New Hampshire
Community Services Council of New
    Hampshire (CSCNH)
79 Sheep Davis Road
Pembroke, NH 03275
Phone: (603) 225-9694
http://www.cscnh.org/

Crossroads House, Inc.
600 Lafayette Road
Portsmouth, NH 03801
Phone: (603) 436-2218
http://www.crossroadshouse.org/

New Jersey
FISH Hospitality Program, Inc.
456 New Market Road
Piscataway, NJ 08854
Phone: (732) 968-5957
http://fishhospitality.com

Interfaith Council for the Homeless
P.O. Box 1494
Morristown, NJ 07962
Phone: (973) 998-0820
http://www.ichfmc.org/

New Mexico
Albuquerque Rescue Mission
2921 Carlisle Blvd., NE
Albuquerque, NM 87110
Phone: (505) 889-6359
http://www.homelessshelterdirectory.org/
cgi-bin/id/shelter.cgi?shelter=8951

Youth Shelters
5686 Agua Fria
Santa Fe, NM 87507
Phone: (505) 983-0586
http://www.youthshelters.org/

New York
The Children's Village
Dobbs Ferry, NY 10522
Phone: (914) 693-0600
http://www.childrensvillage.org/

St. Catherine's Center for Children
40 North Main Avenue
Albany, NY 12203
Phone: (518) 453-6700
http://www.st-cath.org/

North Carolina
Family Services, Inc.
1200 S. Broad Street
Winston-Salem, NC 27101
Phone: (336) 722-8173
http://www.familyserv.org/

Homeless Coalition Day Center
P.O. Box 36296
Fayetteville, NC 28303
Phone: (910) 323-4673

North Dakota
Kedish House of Ellendale
P.O. Box 322
51 First Street North
Ellendale, ND 58436
Phone: (701) 349-4729

Northlands Rescue Mission
420 Division Avenue
Grand Forks, ND 58201
Phone: (701) 772-6609
http://www.northlandsrescuemission.org/

Ohio
Family and Community Services, Inc.
705 Oakwood Street, Suite 221
Ravenna, OH 44266
Phone: (330) 297-7027
http://www.portagefamilies.org/

Haven House
550 High Street
Hamilton, OH 44011
Phone: (513) 863-8866
http://www.havenhouseshelter.org/

Oklahoma
Community Children's Shelter and Family
   Service Center, Inc.
15 Monroe NE
Ardmore, OK 73401
Phone: (580) 226-1838
http://www.childrenshelter.org/

Kid Connections, Inc.
816 South College Avenue
Tahlequah, OK 74464
Phone: (918) 456-3032

Oregon
Goose Hollow Family Shelter
1838 SW Jefferson Street
Portland, OR 97201
Phone: (503) 915-8306
http://www.goosehollowfamilyshelter.org/

Human Solutions
12350 SE Powell Blvd.
Portland, OR 97236
Phone: (503) 548-0200
http://www.humansolutions.org/

Pennsylvania
Community Action Agency
511 Welsh Street
Chester, PA 19013
Phone: (610) 874-8451
http://www.caadc.org/

Family Services Incorporated
2022 Broad Avenue
Altoona, PA 16601
Phone: (814) 944-3583
http://www.familyservicesinc.net/

Rhode Island
Family Resources Community Action
245 Main Street
Woonsocket, RI 02895
Phone: (401) 766-0900
http://famresri.org/

Rhode Island Family Shelter Inc.
165 Beach Avenue
Warwick, RI 02889
Phone: (401) 739-8584
http://www.rifamilyshelter.org

South Carolina
Carolina Youth Development Center
5055 Lackawanna Blvd.
North Charleston, SC 29405
Phone: (843) 266-5200
http://www.cydc.org

Fostering Hope
1001 2nd Avenue
Conway, SC 29526
Phone: (843) 254-8168
http://www.fosteringhopeinc.com/

South Dakota
Mainstream's Homeless Outreach Program
111 North Street
Rapid City, SD 57701
Phone: (605) 343-0650
http://www.behaviormanagement.org/

Missouri Shores Domestic Violence Center
P.O. Box 398
Pierre, SD 57501
Phone: (605) 224-0256
http://www.missourishores.com/

Tennessee
Memphis Family Shelter
P.O. Box 22891
Memphis, TN 38122
Phone: (901) 278-2728
http://www.memphisfamilyshelter.org/

The Salvation Army Care for Kids Program
631 Dickerson Road
Nashville, TN 37207
Phone: (615) 242-0411
http://www.salvationarmyusa.org/usn/
www_usn_2.nsf

Texas
Austin Children's Shelter
4800 Manor Road
Austin, TX 78723
Phone: (512) 499-0090
http://www.austinchildrenshelter.org

Family Gateway
2910 Swiss Avenue
Dallas, TX 75204
Phone: (214) 823-4500
http://www.familygateway.org

Utah
Family Promise of Salt Lake
P.O. Box 996
Salt Lake City, UT 84110
Phone: (801) 961-8622
http://www.fpsl.org/

Rescue Mission of Salt Lake
463 South 400 West
Salt Lake City, UT 84101
Phone: (801) 355-1302
http://www.rescuesaltlake.org/

Vermont
Northeast Kingdom Community Action
   (NEKCA)
P.O. Box 346
70 Main Street
Newport, VT 05855
Phone: (802) 334-7316
http://www.nekca.org/

The Upper Valley Haven
713 Hartford Avenue
White River Junction, VT 05001
Phone: (802) 295-6500
http://www.uppervalleyhaven.org/

Virginia
Carpenter's Shelter
930 North Henry Street
Alexandria, VA 22314
Phone: (703) 548-7500
http://www.carpentersshelter.org/

Katherine K. Hanley Family Shelter
13000 Lee Highway
Fairfax, VA 22030
Phone: (571) 522-6800
http://www.shelterhouse.org/

Washington
Eastside Domestic Violence Program
P.O. Box 6398
Bellevue, WA 98008
Phone: (425) 562-8840
http://www.edvp.org/

Seattle Children's Home
2142 10th Avenue West
Seattle, WA 98119
Phone: (206) 283-3300
http://seattlechildrenshome.org/

West Virginia
Randolph County Homeless Shelter
938 S. Davis Avenue
Elkins, WV 26241
Phone: (304) 636-5193
http://www.ncwvcaa.org/randolph.html

Shenandoah Women's Center
236 W Martin Street
Martinsburg, WV 25401
Phone: (304) 263-8522
http://www.swcinc.org/

Wisconsin
Golden House
1120 University Avenue
Green Bay, WI 54302
Phone: (920) 435-0100
http://www.goldenhousegb.org/

Salvation Army of Dane County
630 E. Washington Avenue
Madison, WI 53703
Phone: (608) 256-2321
http://www.salvationarmydanecounty.org/

Wyoming
Fremont County Good Samaritan Center
917 E Washington Avenue
Riverton, WY 82501
Phone: (307) 856-5435

Sheridan Community Shelter
1898 Fort Road, Building 24
Sheridan, WY 82801
Phone: (307) 673-0025

Further Reading

Books

Clark, Sondra. *77 Creative Ways Kids Can Serve*. Indianapolis: Wesleyan Publishing House, 2008.

Engelmann, Siegfried, Phyllis Haddox, and Elaine Bruner. *Teach Your Child to Read in 100 Easy Lessons*. New York: Fireside, 1986.

Hudson, Orrin C. *One Move at a Time: How to Play and Win at Chess . . . and Life!* Santa Cruz, California: 10 Finger Press, 2007.

Lewis, Barbara. *The Kid's Guide to Service Projects: Over 500 Service Ideas for Young People Who Want to Make a Difference*. Minneapolis: Free Spirit Publishing, 2009.

Nelson, Richard E., Ph.D., Judith C. Galas, and Bev. Cobain, R.N.C. *The Power to Prevent Suicide: A Guide for Teens Helping Teens*. Minneapolis: Free Spirit Publishing, 2006.

Waldman, Jackie. *Teens With the Courage to Give: Young People Who Triumphed over Tragedy and Volunteered to Make a Difference*. Newburyport, Massachusetts: Conari Press, 2000.

Works Consulted

Access Books, http://www.accessbooks.net

Anthony Robbins Foundation, http://anthonyrobbinsfoundation.org

Back to Basics Toys: Name That Toy, http://www.backtobasicstoys.com/trivia/

The Care Bags Foundation, http://www.carebags4kids.org

"Carnival Game Ideas," http://www.schoolcarnivals.com/Games/alphabetical.htm

Cookbook Publishers, Inc., Fund-raising Cookbooks, http://www.cookbookpublishers.com/

Free Rice, http://www.freerice.com

Gateway Cookbook Publishers: *Fund-raising Cookbooks*, http://www.gatebook.com/

The Green Teen Community Gardening Program, http://www.greenteen.org

"Homemade Carnival Games Ideas," http://ezinearticles.com/?Homemade-Carnival-Games-Ideas&id=1305683

"How to Be a Peer Counselor," http://www.ehow.com/how_2146602_be-peer-counselor.html

"How to Make a Quillow," http://www.straw.com/quilting/articles/quillows.html

Lucy Gardens, "Sensory Garden for Kids," http://www.lucygardens.com/sensory-garden-for-kids.html

Marine Toys for Tots Foundation, http://www.toysfortots.org

Online Literacy Activities, http://www.boardman.k12.oh.us/bdms/golubic/onlineliteracy.htm

"Phillies' Rollins and Pals Create Major Memories for Kids." *Philadelphia Daily News*, July 24, 2009. http://www.prosportsdaily.com/comments/rollins-and-pals-create-major-memories-for-kids-257587.html

Robbins, Anthony. "Five Keys to Thrive." *Change Your Life Now*, http://tonyrobbinstraining.com/378/5-keys-to-thrive/

Share Literacy, http://www.shareliteracy.org

Stone, Gigi. "Beware of Fraud When Making Charitable Donations," *ABC News*, December 25, 2005. http://abcnews.go.com/WNT/Business/story?id=1441720

PHOTO CREDITS: Cover, pp. 5, 6–8, 10, 12, 15, 16, 19, 20, 26, 29, 33, 39—Creative Commons 2.0; pp. 1, 34, 37—David Handschuh/Jupiter Images; p. 24—Getty Images. Every effort has been made to locate all copyright holders of material used in this book. If any errors or omissions have occurred, corrections will be made in future editions of the book.

Index

Laya Saul has been involved with community service from a young age. She has taught first aid and CPR for the Red Cross, volunteered with youth, and started community organizations that serve and educate their members. She has been involved with various charities and has seen firsthand the good that can come from donating time and money to worthy causes.

Laya is also known to lots of people as Aunt Laya because she wrote a book for teens (called *You Don't Have to Learn Everything the Hard Way*) to help them live happier, safer lives.

Born in Los Angeles, California, she now lives gratefully with her husband, kids, dog, and cat in Israel.